A SPIRITUAL DOG "BEAR"

A SPIRITUAL DOG "BEAR"

Jay W. Porter

CHOSE YOUR LOVE
JOY NO MATTER WHAT

Printed in the United States of America

This story began in Killeen, TX on 3 January 2003 at the Killeen Second Chance Animal Shelter.

6

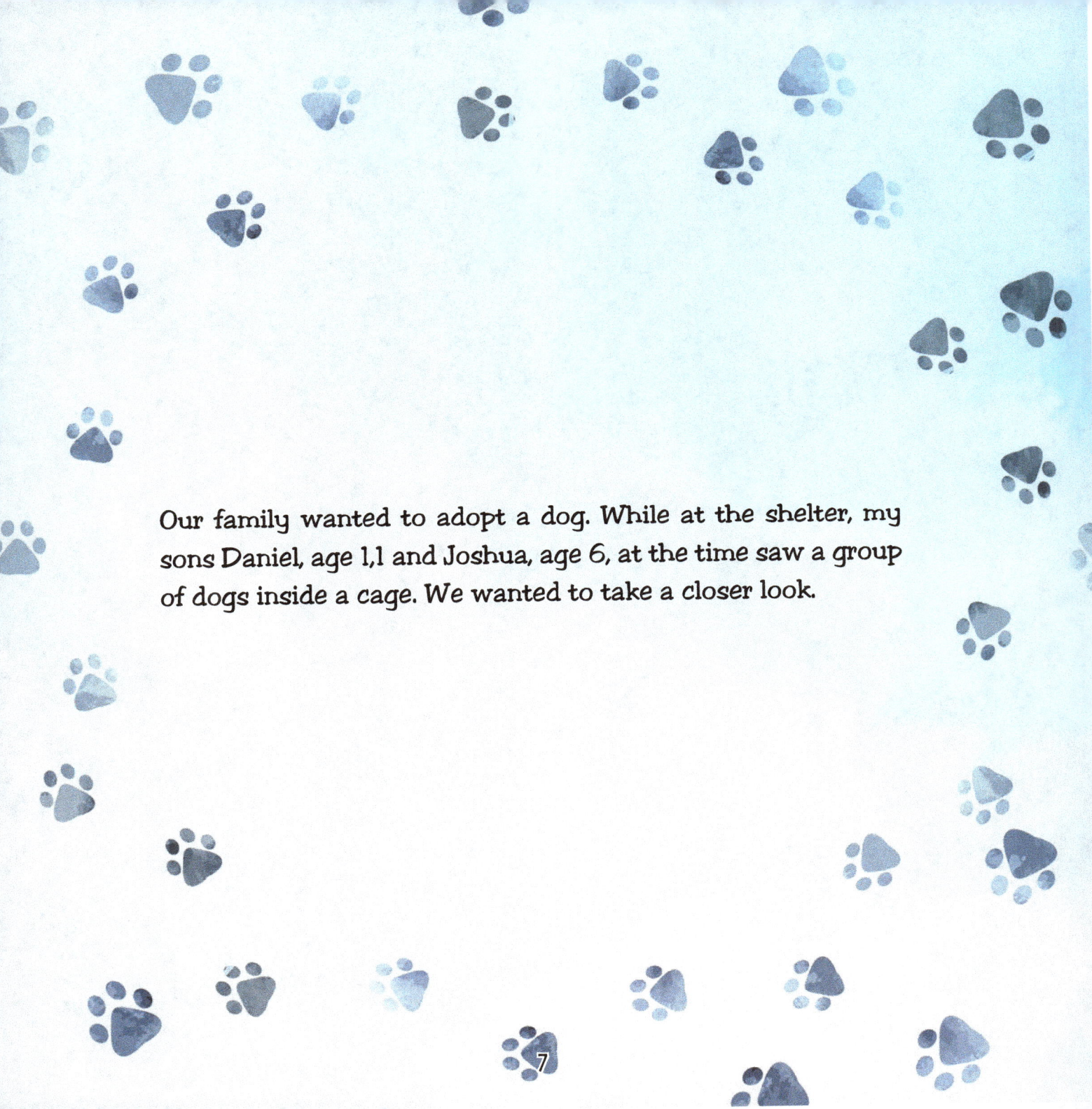

Our family wanted to adopt a dog. While at the shelter, my sons Daniel, age 1,1 and Joshua, age 6, at the time saw a group of dogs inside a cage. We wanted to take a closer look.

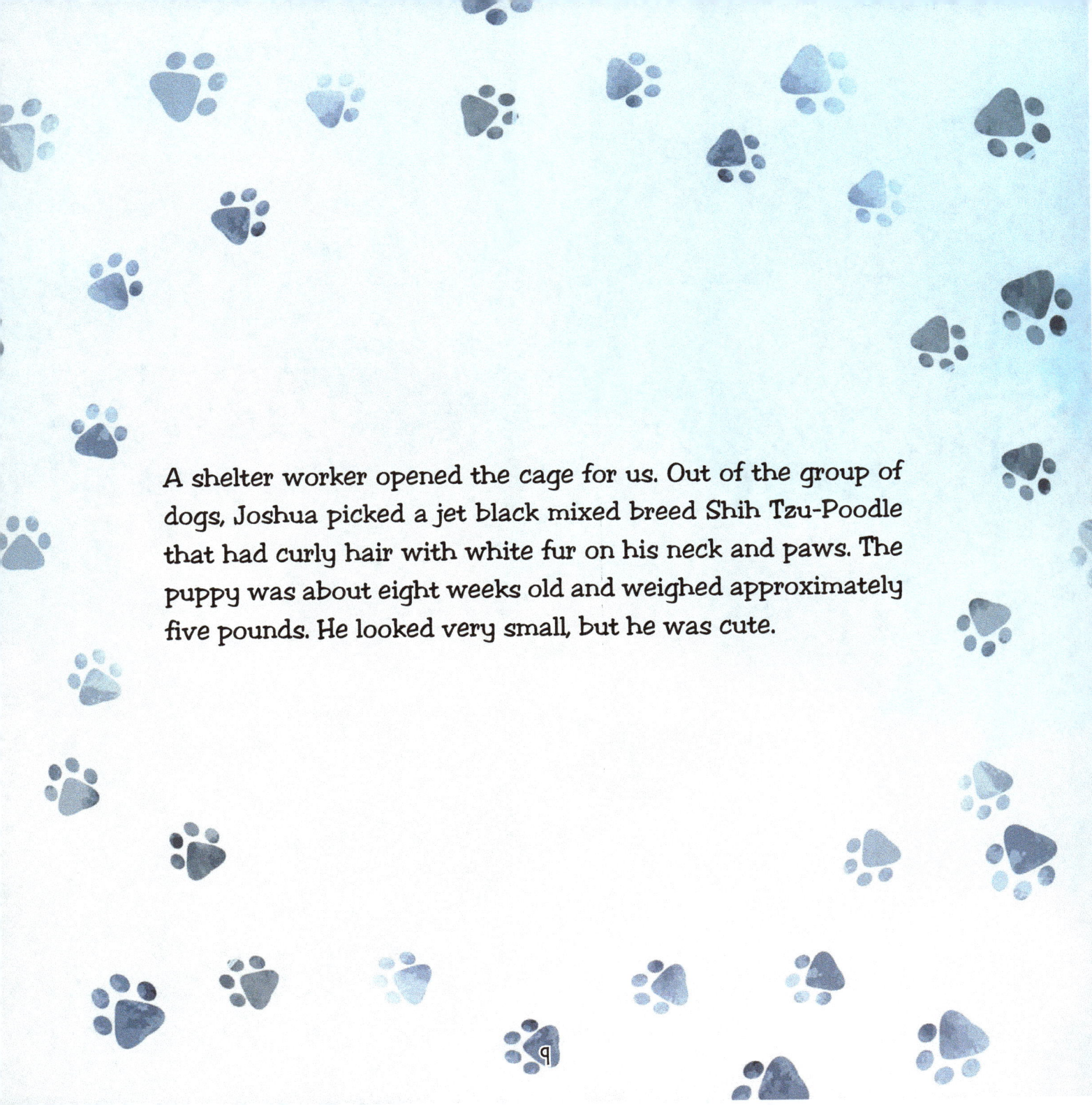

A shelter worker opened the cage for us. Out of the group of dogs, Joshua picked a jet black mixed breed Shih Tzu-Poodle that had curly hair with white fur on his neck and paws. The puppy was about eight weeks old and weighed approximately five pounds. He looked very small, but he was cute.

We really liked this dog. When the puppy licked my hand, we all knew he was the one for us. His given name was Bear. We took Bear home with our family to his new environment.

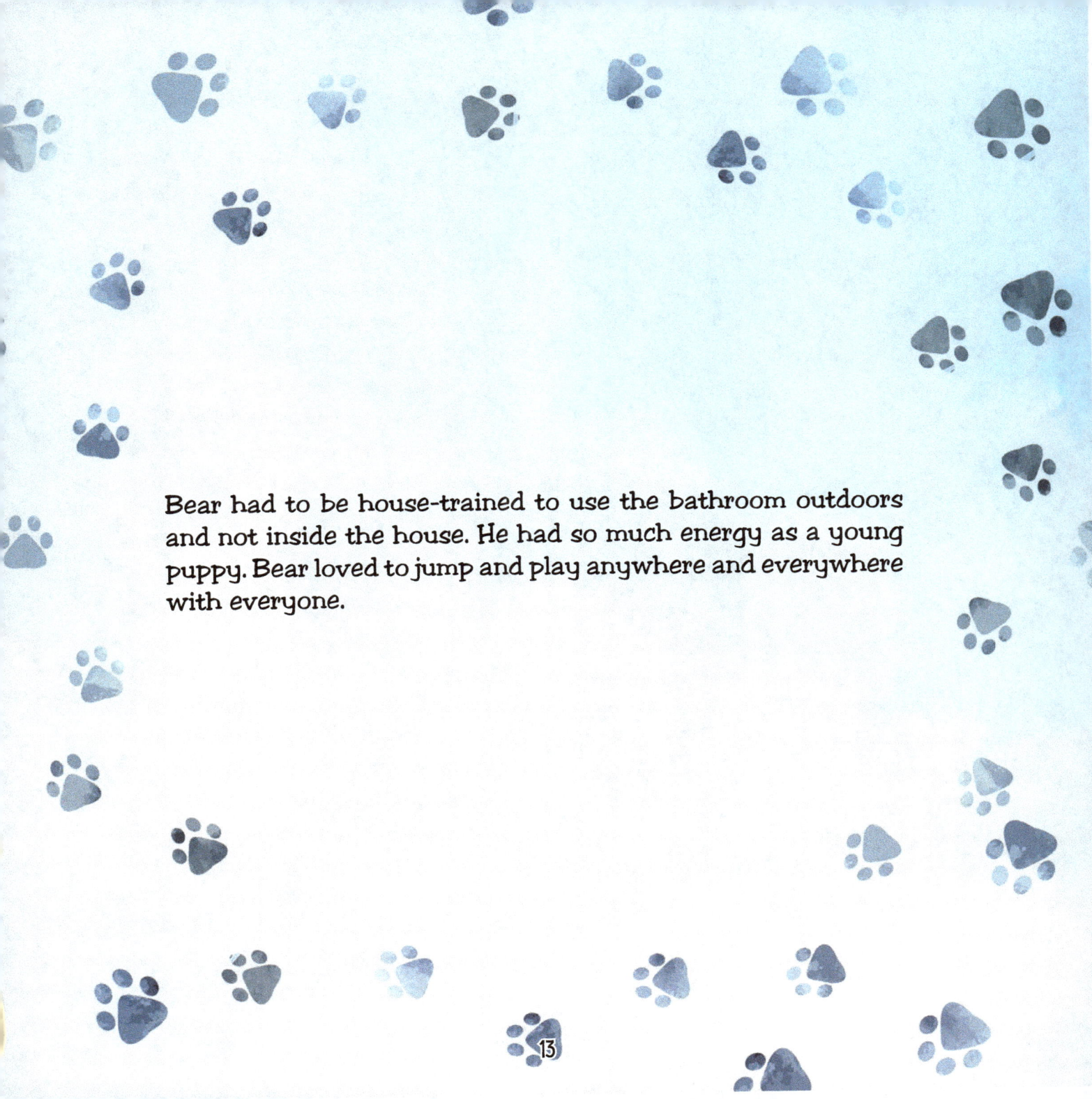

Bear had to be house-trained to use the bathroom outdoors and not inside the house. He had so much energy as a young puppy. Bear loved to jump and play anywhere and everywhere with everyone.

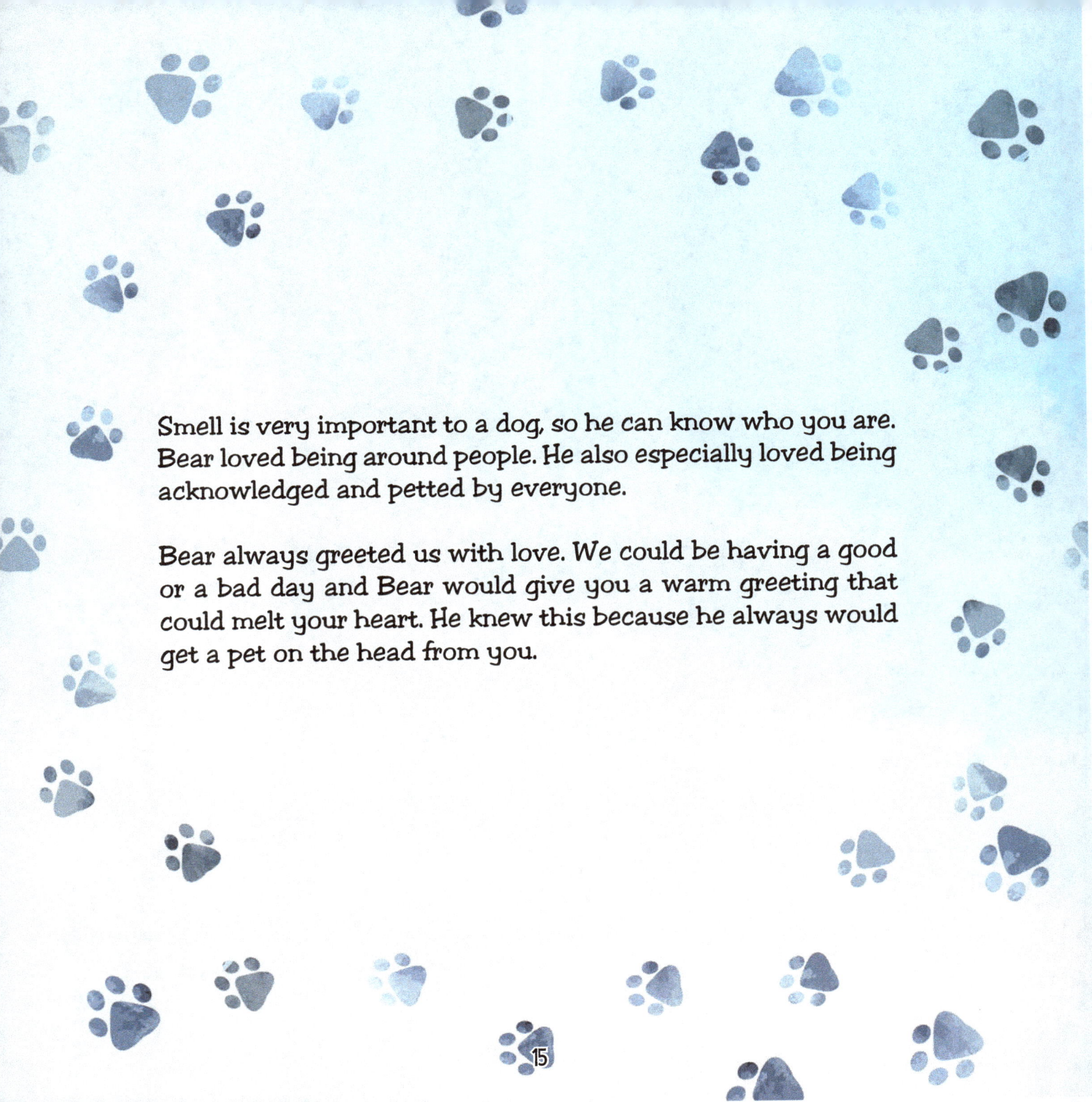

Smell is very important to a dog, so he can know who you are. Bear loved being around people. He also especially loved being acknowledged and petted by everyone.

Bear always greeted us with love. We could be having a good or a bad day and Bear would give you a warm greeting that could melt your heart. He knew this because he always would get a pet on the head from you.

Bear loved smelling and walking in his territory inside the house and outside the house in the front and back yard. He also had another passion; He loved to eat.

Bear weighed five pounds and was about eight- weeks old when we brought him home from the animal shelter. By the time he was three years old, he reached twenty-eight pounds, the adult size of a mixed breed Shih Tzu-Poodle.

Bear had a team of awesome groomers. They gave him haircuts, trimmed his paws, and he received nice baths. Each time I went to pick Bear up from the groomers, he was always happy and looked great.

As Bear gotten older, his fur color started changing from jet-black to grayish white. When his hair grew, it would be very shaggy and curly. Every two to three months, we knew it was time for Bear to get a haircut and grooming.

The place we took Bear for grooming was the local Killeen Animal Care Center. We also take Bear there whenever our family needed to leave the local area, They provide boarding services and care for dogs, cats, and other pets.

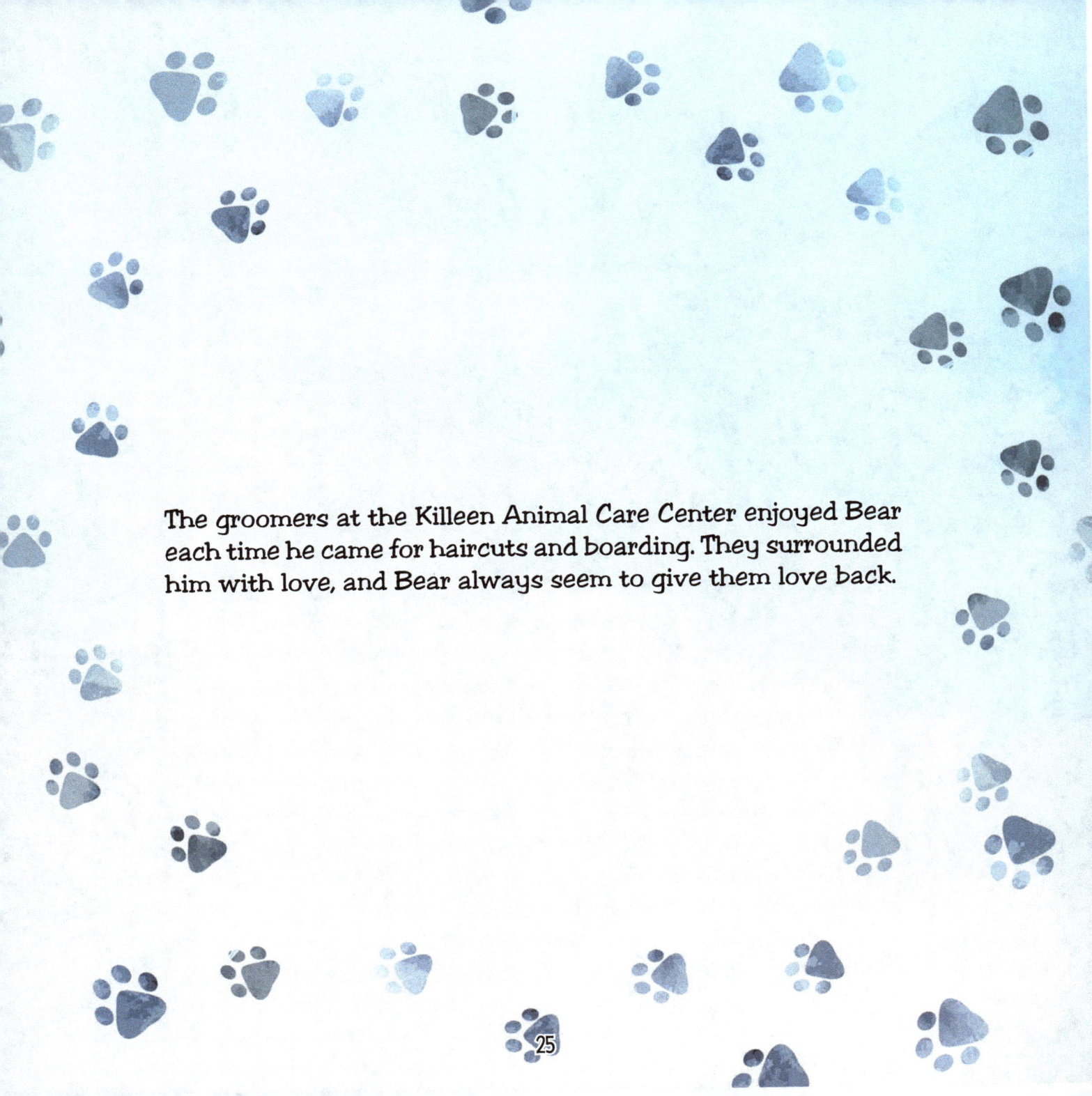

The groomers at the Killeen Animal Care Center enjoyed Bear each time he came for haircuts and boarding. They surrounded him with love, and Bear always seem to give them love back.

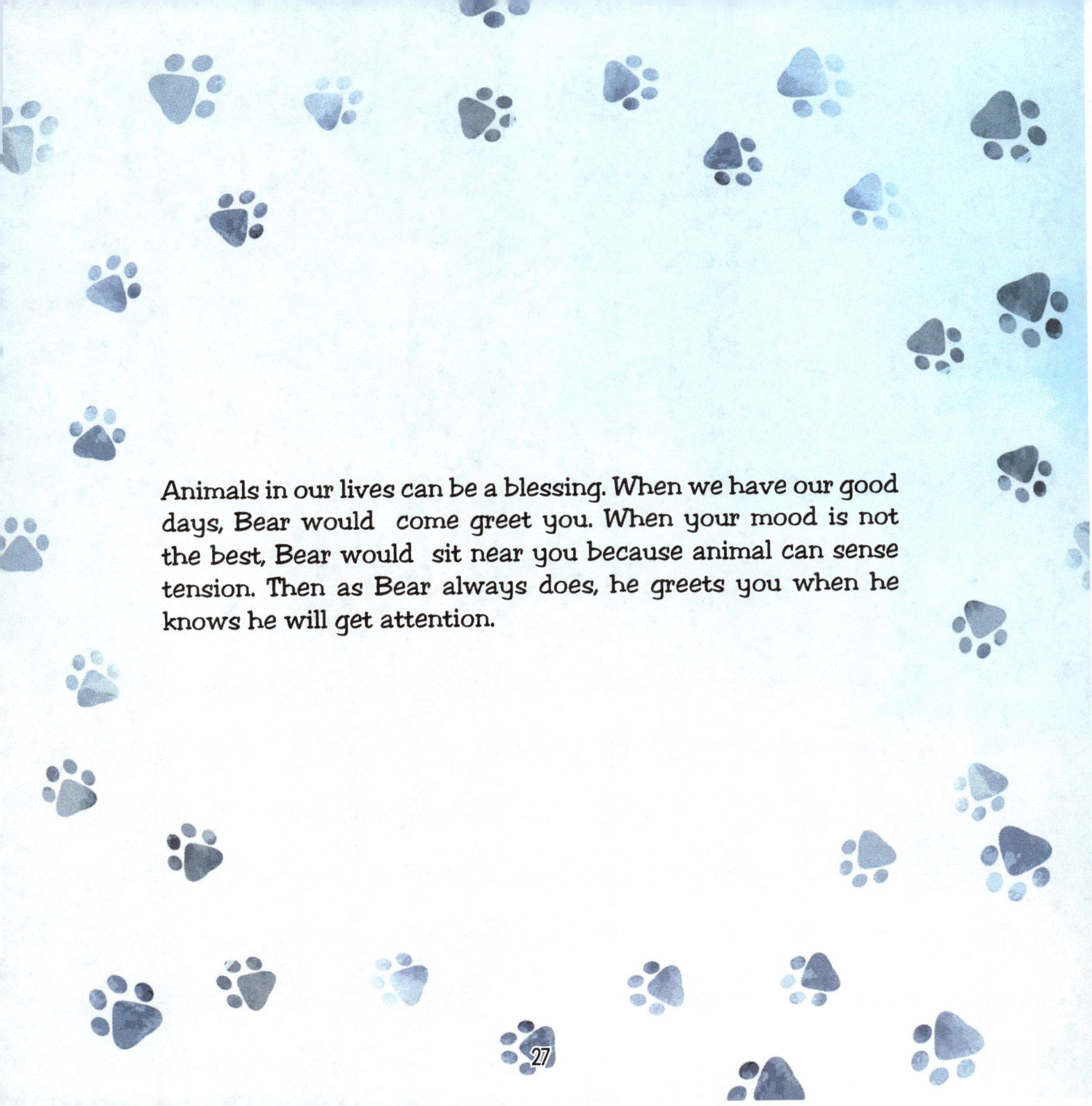

Animals in our lives can be a blessing. When we have our good days, Bear would come greet you. When your mood is not the best, Bear would sit near you because animal can sense tension. Then as Bear always does, he greets you when he knows he will get attention.

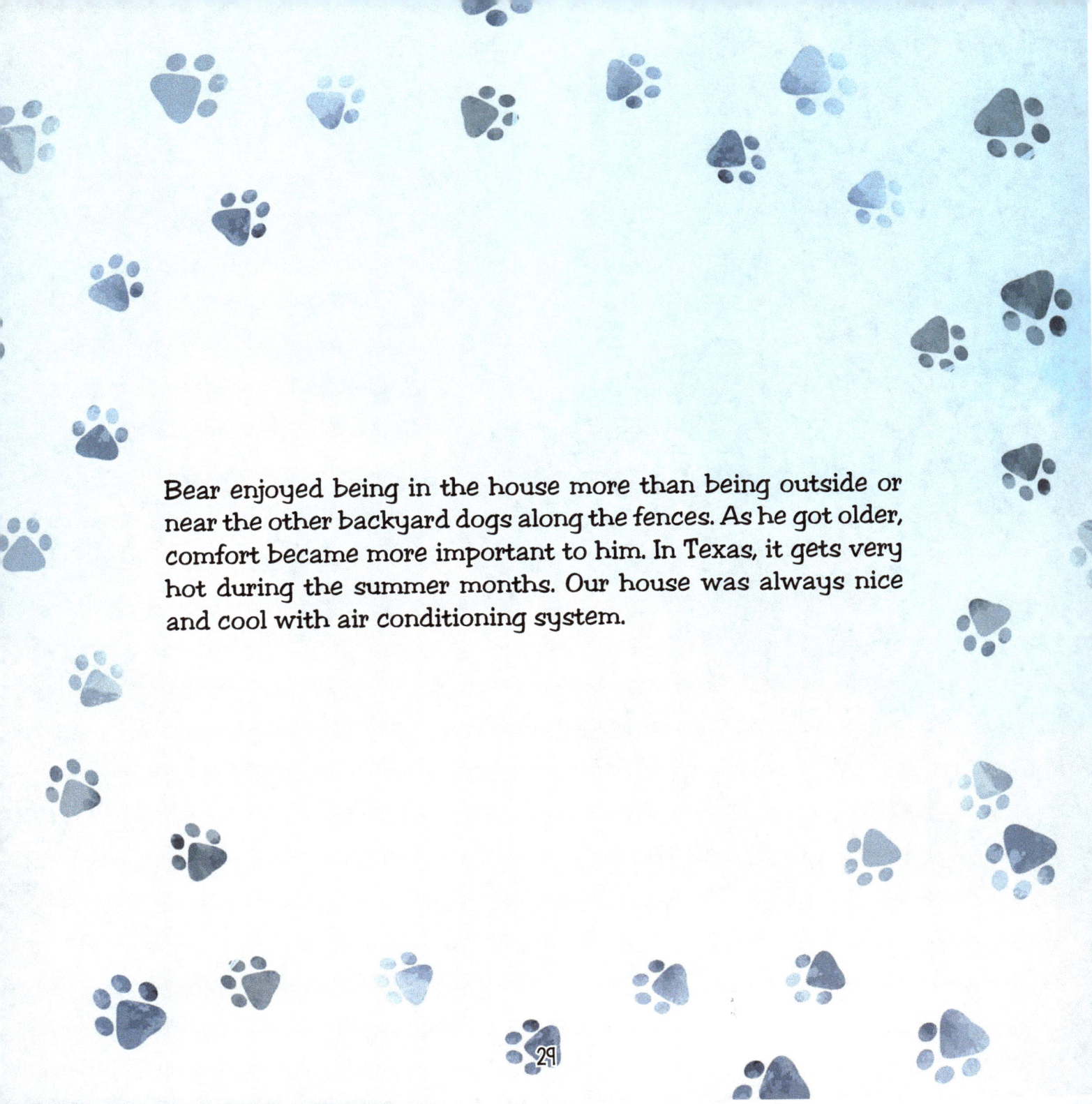

Bear enjoyed being in the house more than being outside or near the other backyard dogs along the fences. As he got older, comfort became more important to him. In Texas, it gets very hot during the summer months. Our house was always nice and cool with air conditioning system.

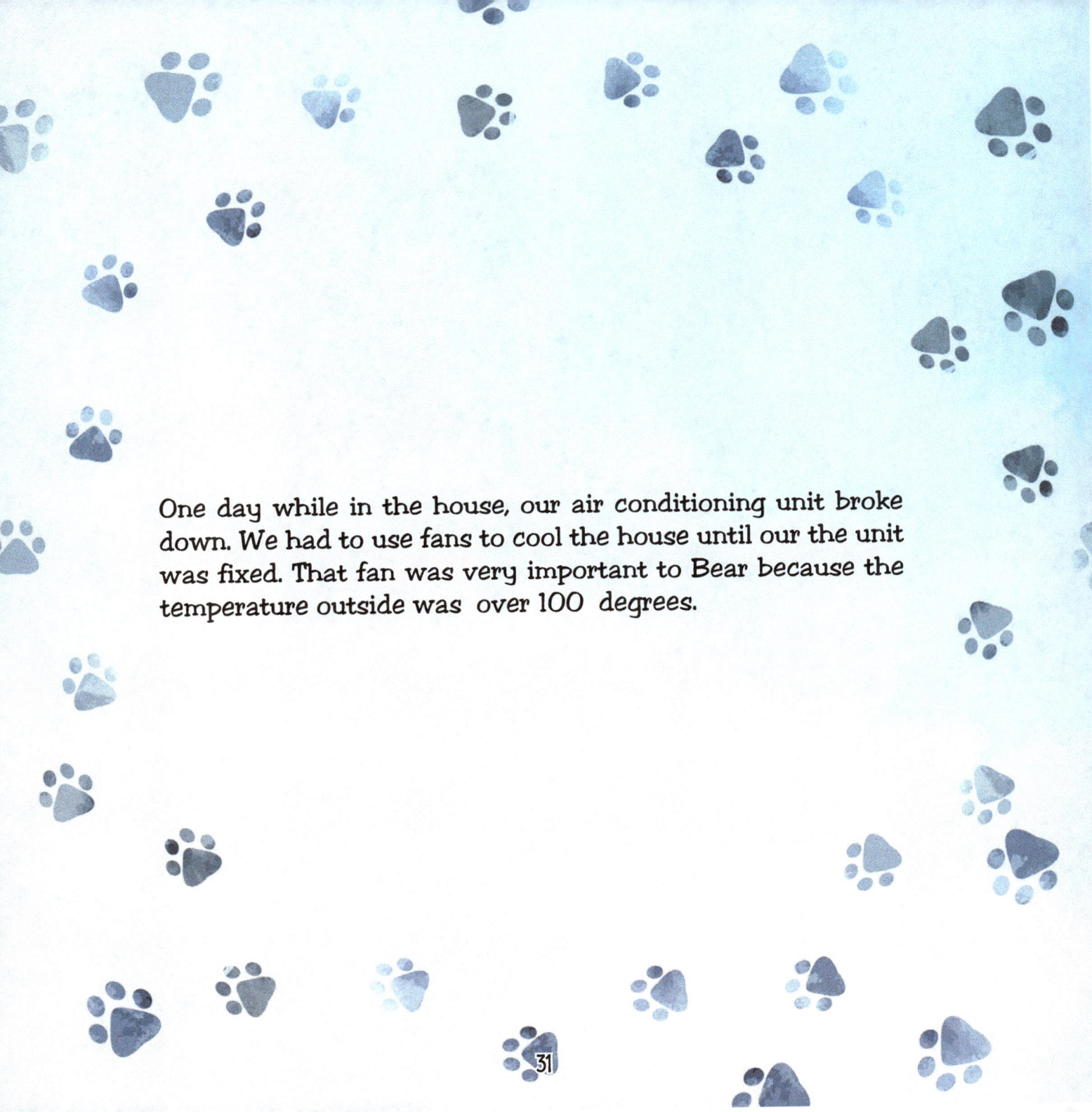

One day while in the house, our air conditioning unit broke down. We had to use fans to cool the house until our the unit was fixed. That fan was very important to Bear because the temperature outside was over 100 degrees.

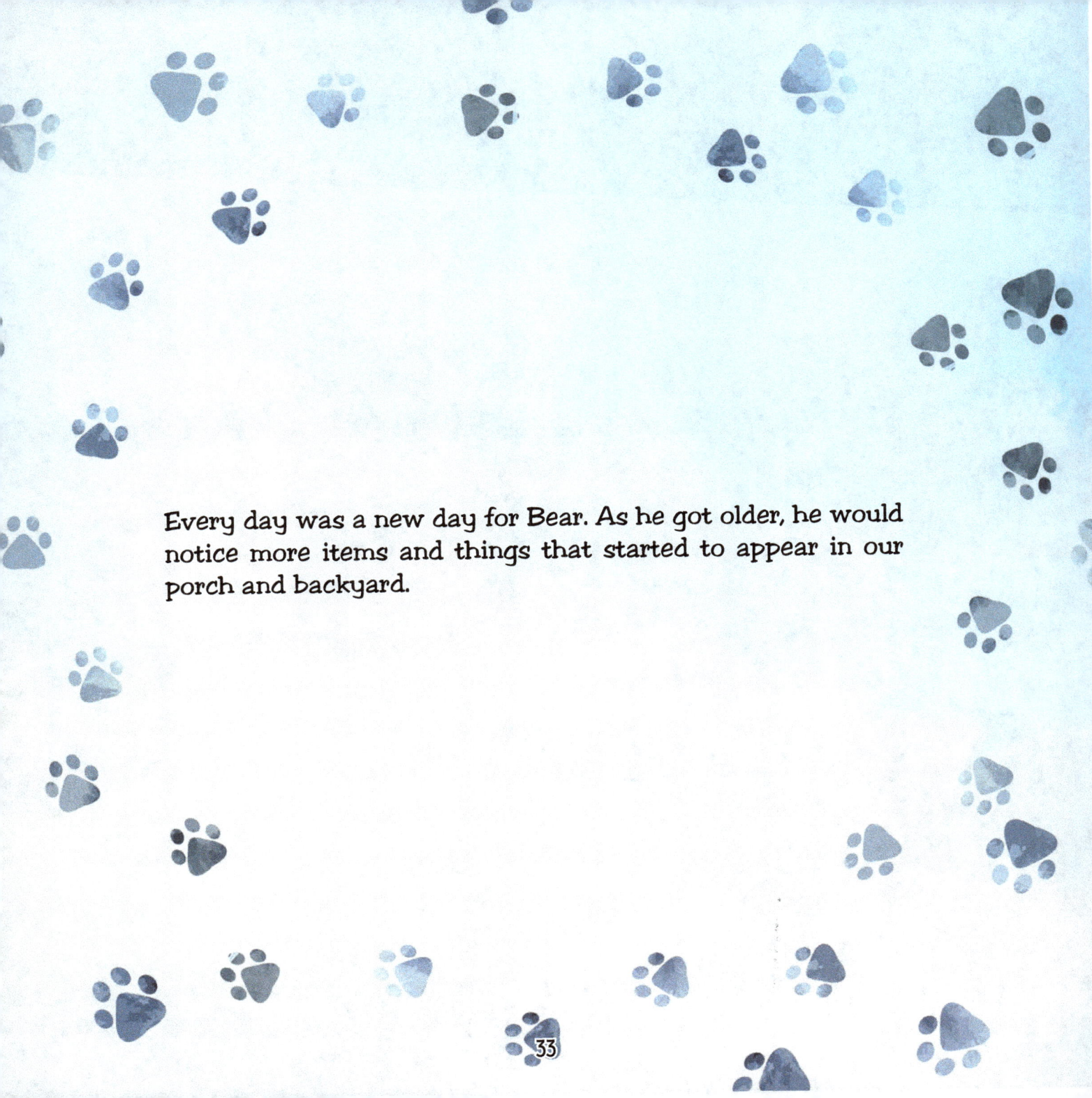

Every day was a new day for Bear. As he got older, he would notice more items and things that started to appear in our porch and backyard.

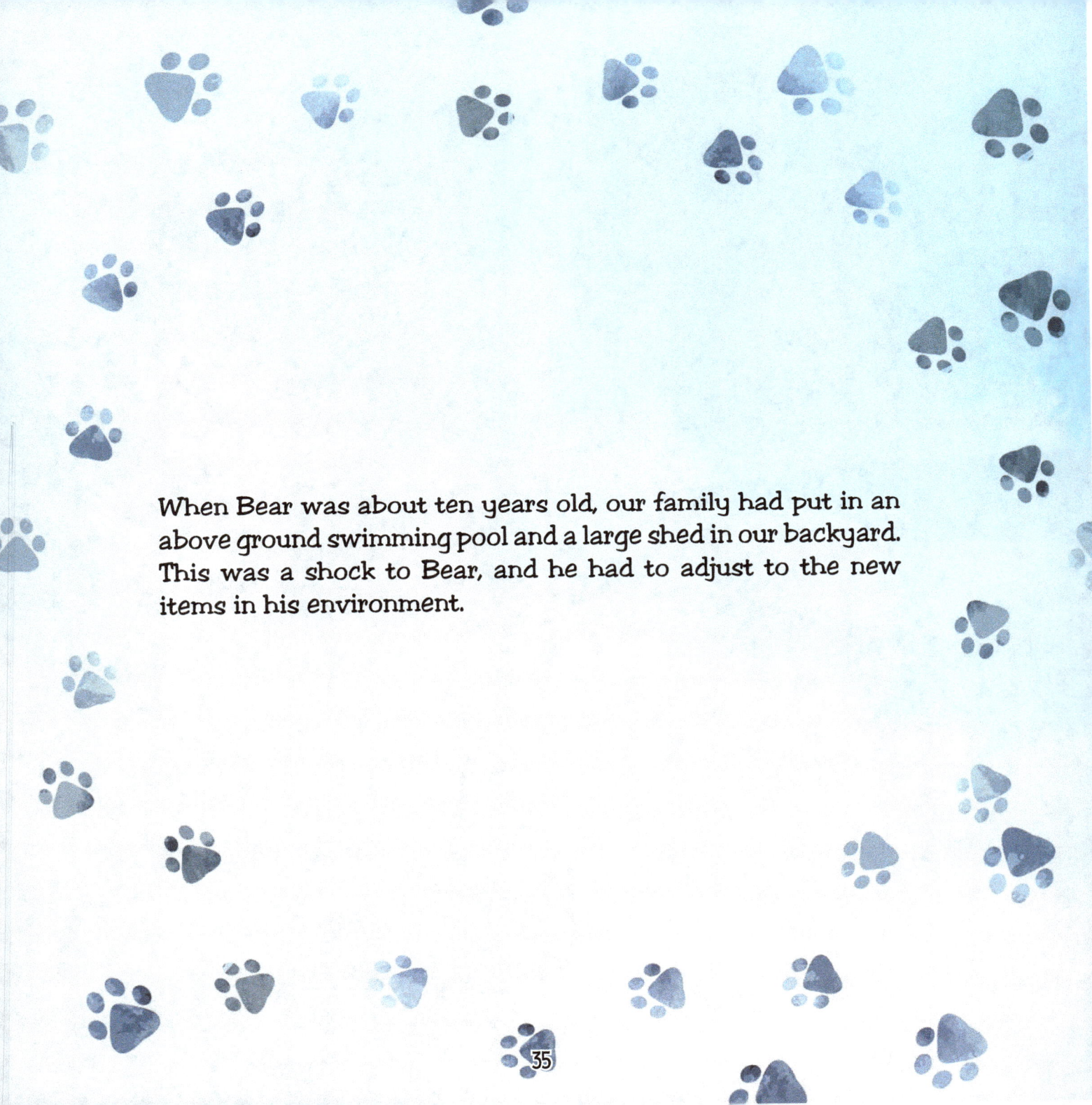

When Bear was about ten years old, our family had put in an above ground swimming pool and a large shed in our backyard. This was a shock to Bear, and he had to adjust to the new items in his environment.

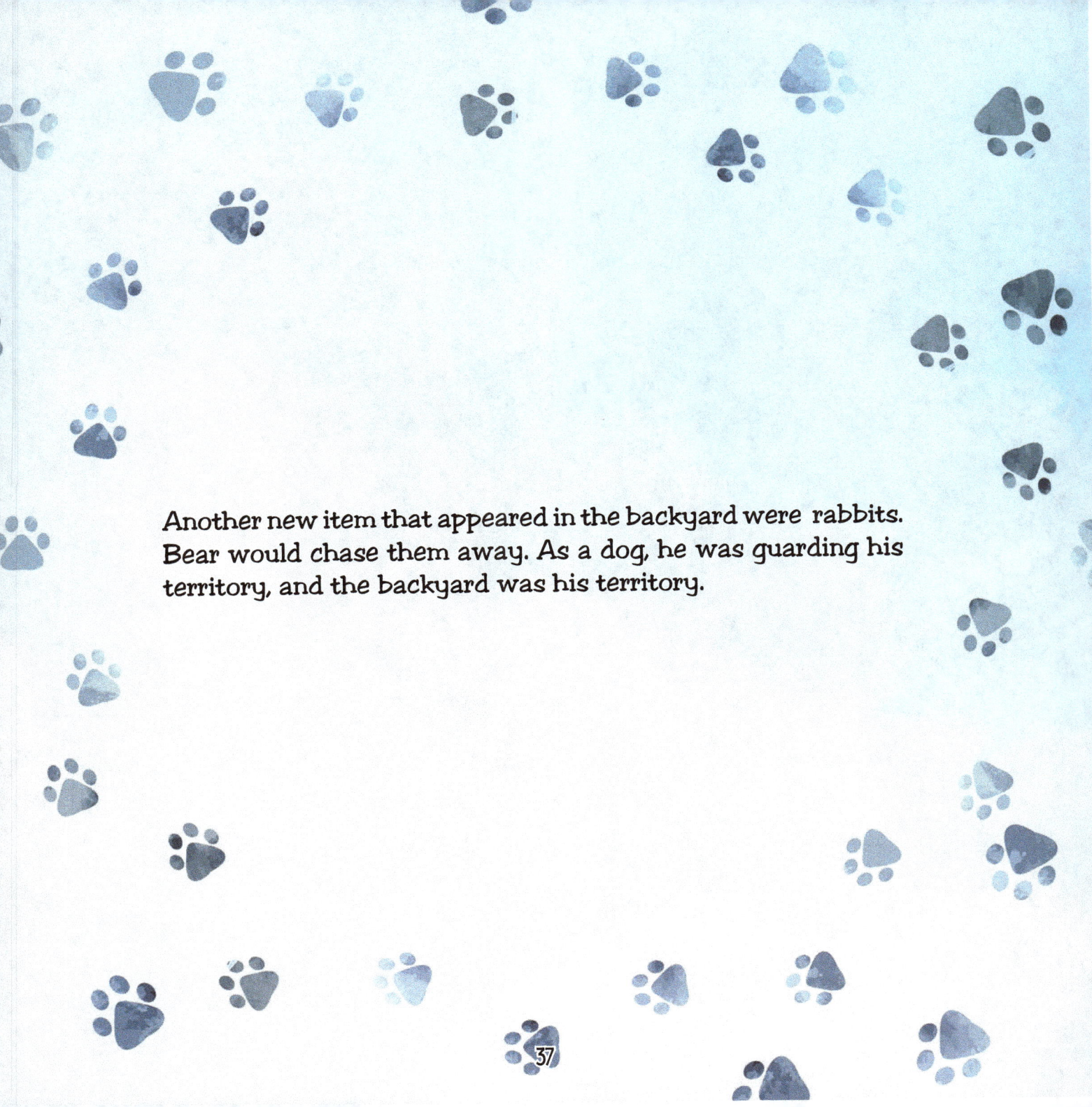

Another new item that appeared in the backyard were rabbits. Bear would chase them away. As a dog, he was guarding his territory, and the backyard was his territory.

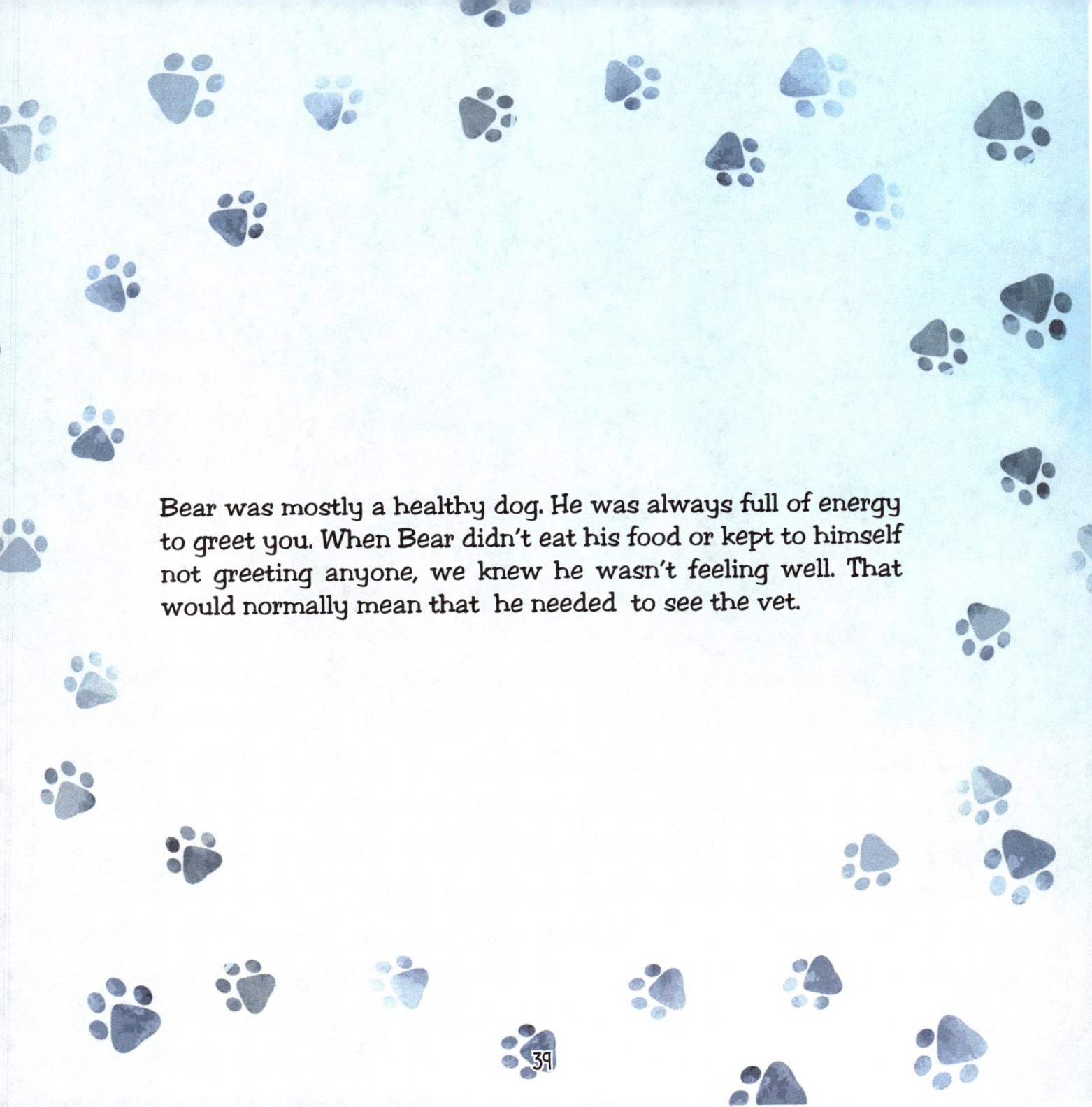

Bear was mostly a healthy dog. He was always full of energy to greet you. When Bear didn't eat his food or kept to himself not greeting anyone, we knew he wasn't feeling well. That would normally mean that he needed to see the vet.

About the time Bear was twelve years old, he began to not move as fast as he used to. He still enjoyed people and always wanted his petting and acknowledgement from you. Bear made sure you knew he was there.

Bear started to show signs of aging, because sometimes he used the bathroom in the house and didn't make it outside. Sometimes you would call his name and he would not hear you because his hearing was going bad. Bear also had pain in his legs and back causing him to move slower.

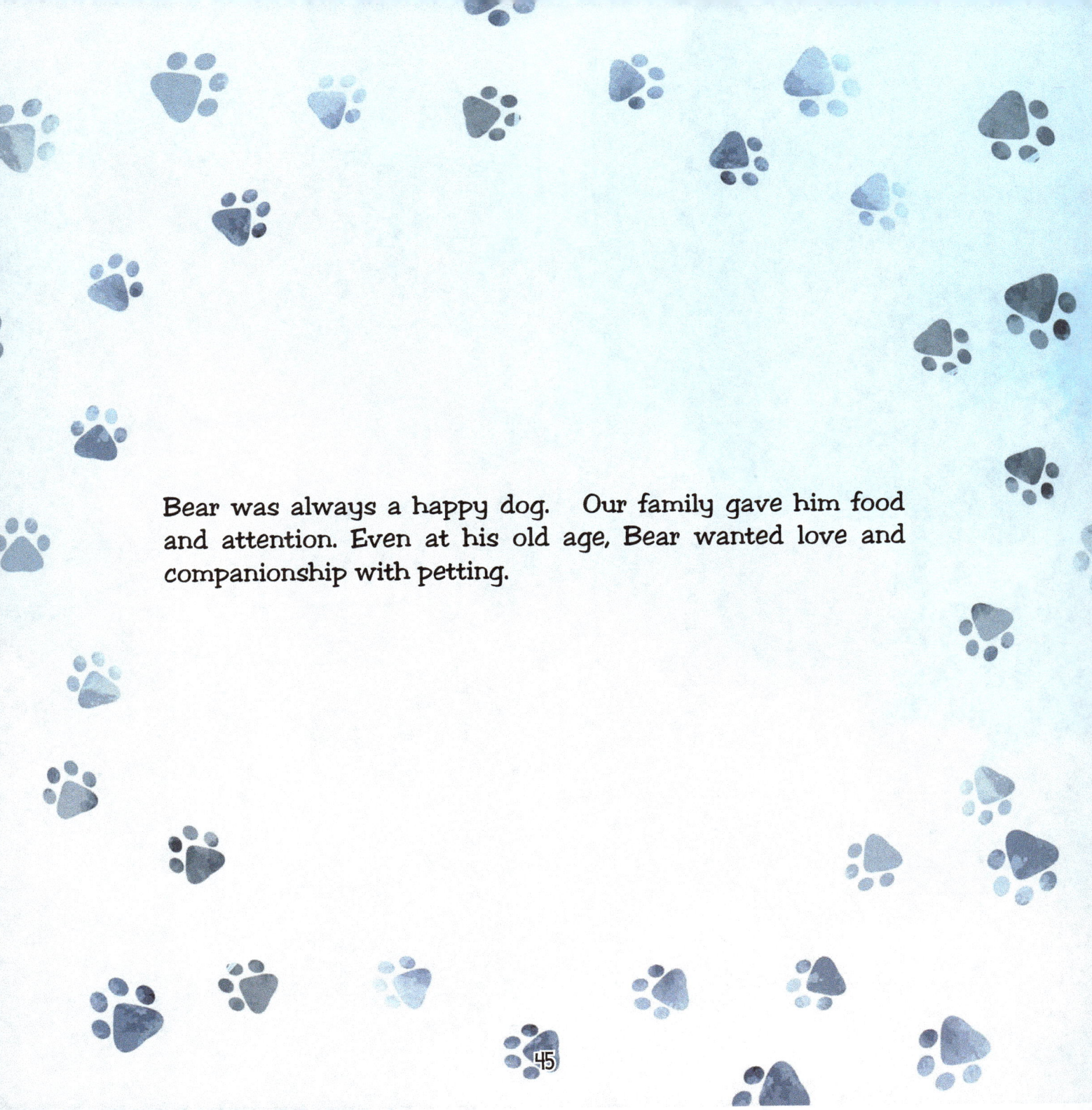

Bear was always a happy dog.   Our family gave him food and attention. Even at his old age, Bear wanted love and companionship with petting.

One day, Bear was sitting outside the screened porch in the backyard in the sunlight. He hasn't eaten in two days or drank any water. Bear was having issues with pain and not greeting anyone. He was not himself at all. Bear's breathing was very fast and rapid. I knew it was time to take him to the animal hospital.

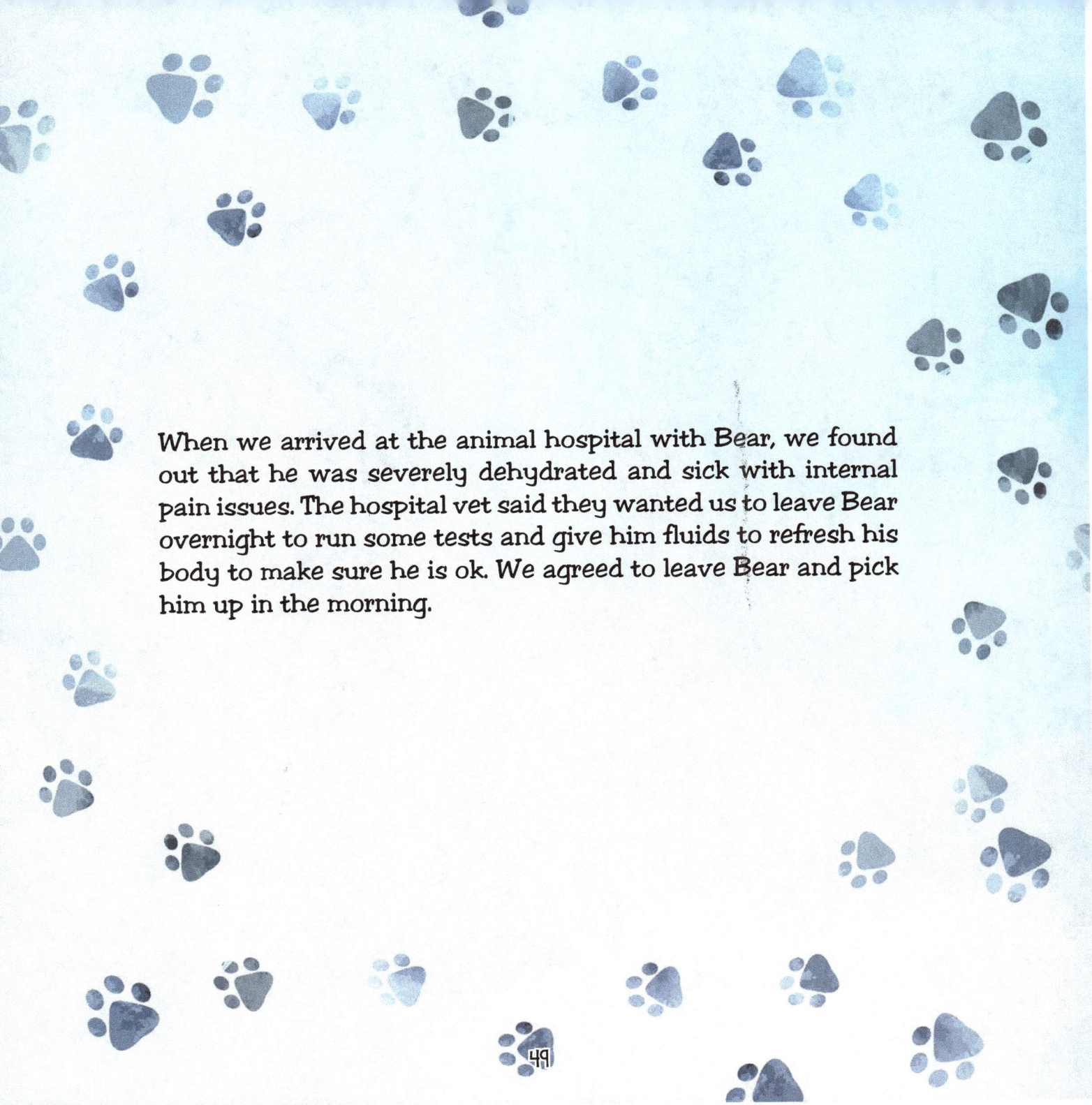

When we arrived at the animal hospital with Bear, we found out that he was severely dehydrated and sick with internal pain issues. The hospital vet said they wanted us to leave Bear overnight to run some tests and give him fluids to refresh his body to make sure he is ok. We agreed to leave Bear and pick him up in the morning.

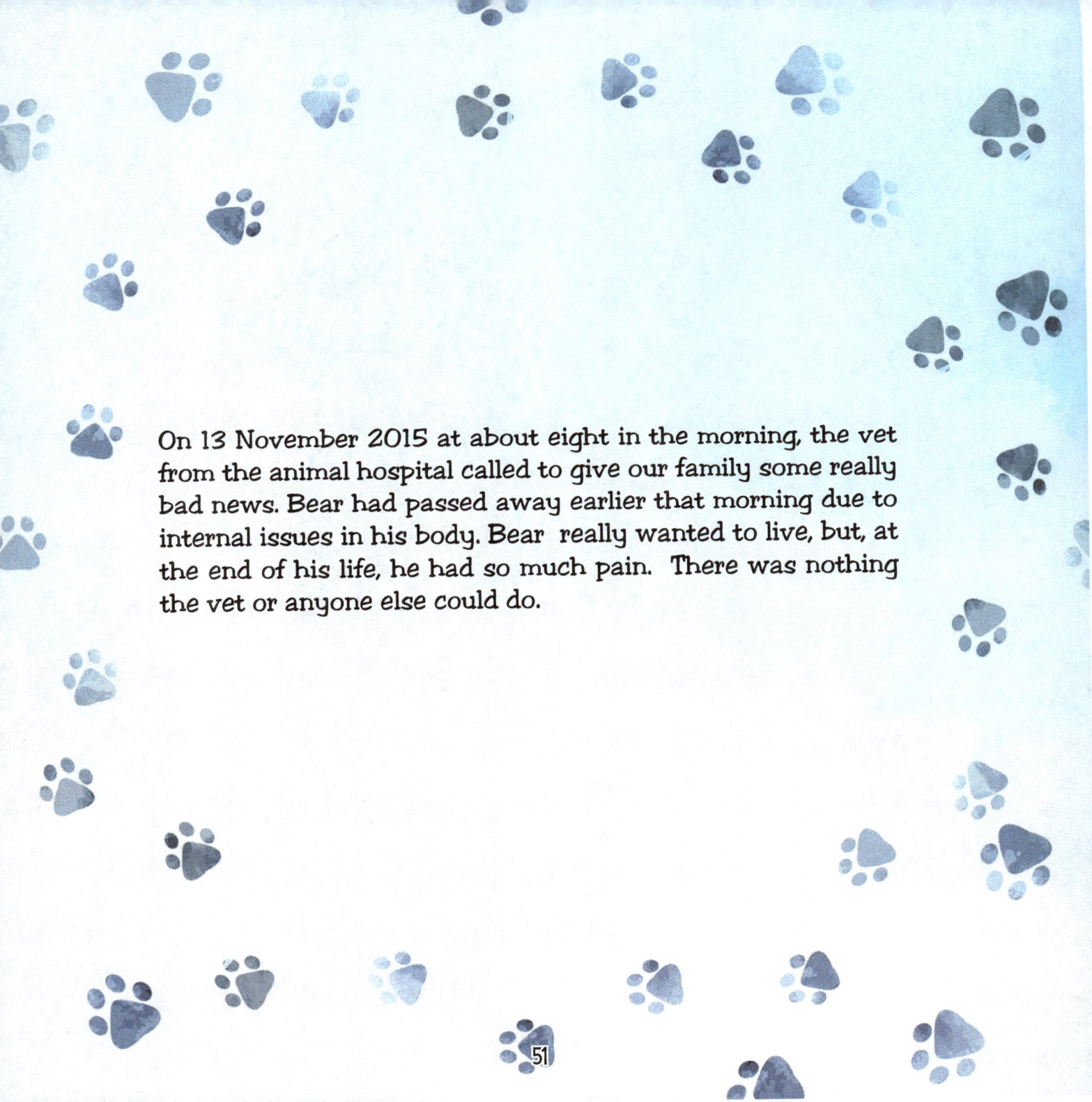

On 13 November 2015 at about eight in the morning, the vet from the animal hospital called to give our family some really bad news. Bear had passed away earlier that morning due to internal issues in his body. Bear really wanted to live, but, at the end of his life, he had so much pain. There was nothing the vet or anyone else could do.

Bear's death was hard to believe. Our house with Bear was once very lively and noisy with energy is now very quiet. The news of Bear's passing was hard on my sons Daniel now twenty-four and Joshua now nineteen.

Our family tried the best we could to give Bear a good life. We were blessed for thirteen years with the opportunity to enjoy a beautiful dog who was special. The family will always remember Bear in our hearts. In this life, we don't always realize what we have until it is gone. Be kind to all pets and animals because they will be kind back to you.